F

ECH D
SH

Tales and Traditions of Newport and Nevern

Brian John

Greencroft Books
2008

Preface

Ten years ago I published a little book called *Beneath the Mountain.* It sold out very quickly, and because I had other priorities at the time it was never reprinted. I have had many requests for a new edition, and at last the matter has come to the top of my priorities list. This new book is a substantial revision of the old one, with much new text material and many new illustrations. I have also given the book a new title, based on two ideas -- namely that tales and traditions are kept alive because people hear echoes from the past and respond to them positively, and that the landscape itself is full of shadows which emphasize and exaggerate buildings and monuments and give us clues to what has gone before. If we can keep alive the habits of listening and looking carefully, we are much more likely to value and protect that strange thing called "heritage" for future generations.

So it is the purpose of this little book to record just a few of the strange things that feature in the past and present of the parishes of Newport and Nevern -- and in so doing, to help in ensuring that they remain firmly fixed in the consciousness of local people and visitors alike. After all, the things that make this little corner of Wales so fascinating are not just its fresh air, soaring skies and rugged landscapes, but its unique buildings, its strange traditions, its novelties and its eccentricities.

Newport parish church, with its Norman tower

Introduction

The countryside around Newport and Nevern contains, in its landscape and structures, traces of a long and fascinating history. The two parishes lie at the core of the old Barony of Cemais. Newport parish has a compact shape, extending as far south as Llannerch in Cwm Gwaun and from Brithdir in the east to Mynydd Melyn in the west. Nevern is the largest parish in Pembrokeshire, stretching all the way from the coast near Moylgrove to Foel Eryr and Foel Feddau on Myndd Preseli.

There are signs of a Mesolithic (Middle Stone Age) flint-working floor on the estuary near Newport, but the earliest visible man-made features date from the New Stone Age. These include the massive cromlechs or burial chambers of Pentre Ifan and Carreg Coetan Arthur. In the Bronze Age, around 3,000 years ago, people lived and herded their cattle and sheep on the stony slopes of Carningli, and left traces of their enclosures and settlement sites. In the Iron Age, before the time of Christ, there were villages or smaller fortified sites used by family groups on Carningli, Carnffoi, Castell Henllys and elsewhere. And later, as the population grew, Welsh and Irish tribal groups cleared the primeval forest, struggled over territory, and gradually tamed the landscape with the arts and crafts of agriculture. Christian mystics and monks (including the local hero St Brynach) founded small monastic communities, for example at Nevern, during the "Age of the Saints".

Stone quays and old warehouse on the Parrog

Then things started to get complicated. The Vikings probably knew the coast of Newport Bay, but no trace has ever been found of their visits. Later, the arrival of the Normans led to centuries of social upheaval, with motte and bailey and stone castles being built by both the Welsh princes and the invaders during the ebbs and flows of their military campaigns. Newport Castle became a key fortress. The main invisible product of this time was the Barony of Cemais, which survives to this day. The founding of the port on the the Nevern Estuary, and the first use of the name "Newport", came in the early Middle Ages. The Parrog gradually developed as the home of a small seafaring community. A short distance inland, the Norman town developed under the protection of the castle battlements, with streets running downslope towards the shore and with more than 200 burgage plots occupied by burgesses or freemen. There were at least three water mills within the town boundaries, and more than a fair share of inns.

Schools and chapels came later, built during the social and evangelical transformations of the eighteenth and nineteenth centuries. Later still merchants, craftsmen, shopkeepers, doctors and bankers, teachers and "lodging-house proprietors" all helped to change the face of the town. Today, Newport still carries the proud title of "Ancient Borough" and it is still (to the amusement of the locals) the main seat of feudal power in Pembrokeshire. The medieval layout of the town can still be appreciated, and it is still dominated by its castle and tall-towered parish church.

The smaller settlements of Nevern, Brynberian and Cilgwyn have changed very little over the centuries. Nevern, with its motte and bailey castle, and its Celtic Cross and ancient church settled in a gentle valley, has a timeless quality which strikes every visitor. Like the clustered hamlet of Brynberian and the scattered hamlet of Cilgwyn, it has grown hardly at all over 500 years. But this is far from being a derelict landscape, and partly because of its location within the National Park many newcomers (including young families) have moved in to take the place of the old farming families which have died out or moved out in response to changing economic circumstances.

In the modern Newport a number of old traditions still survive, possibly because (like Laugharne on the coast of Carmarthen Bay) there is great social stability here and a small enough population to ensure that multinational corporations have not been tempted to move in! With only about 1,000 people in the town, some very ancient families, a fascinating social structure, a multitude of clubs and committees, a singular lack of respect for authority and a reputation for rugged individuality if not ill-discipline, the modern town is a wonderful and eccentric place. Among its assets are a splendid community spirit, a clean and beautiful environment, and a continuing respect for some rather idiosyncratic traditions like the Beating of the Bounds, the Pwnc and Plygain, the game of Cnapan, the Court Leet and Ffair Gurig. Mystified? Well, read on......

Traditions and Relics

The Nevern Valley Cromlechs

The broad and gentle slopes around the Nevern Valley support one of the most important concentrations of "cromlechs" (Neolithic burial chambers) in the British Isles. We do not know how many there were originally, but six of them, in various stages of disrepair, can still be seen: at Pentre Ifan not far from Tycanol Wood, at Carreg Coetan Arthur in Newport, at Cerrig y Gof west of Newport, at Trellyffaint north of Nevern, at Llech y Dribedd to the southwest of Moylgrove, and at Bedd yr Afanc in the tributary valley of Afon Brynberian.

The chambered tombs or graves are about 5,000 years old, and they show a great mastery of the "megalithic" technique of building with large slabs of rock. No particular rock type was favoured over any other,

Pentre Ifan portal dolmen or cromlech -- the most famous Neolithic site in Wales

Carreg Coetan Arthur, Newport

and the builders always used locally available stones and boulders; there was no long-distance transport. Indeed, the builders may have located some of their cromlechs in spots where large flattish boulders were readily available in the form of glacial erratics or rocky outcrops.

The most famous cromlech in Wales is Pentre Ifan, which because of its slender grace and sheer size is now one of the key "heritage" destinations of the UK; but Carreg Coetan Arthur and Llech y Dribedd are also very impressive. Perhaps the most interesting, from an archaeological point of view, are Cerrig y Gof and Bedd yr Afanc. The former (in a field adjacent to the Newport-Dinas road) is very unusual in that there are actually five burial chambers clustered together on the same site, and the latter is a long "gallery grave" unique in Wales.

Inevitably, there are old traditions associated with the cromlechs. In the sixteenth century they were thought to have been built by giants. Later they were thought to have been the sacred sites used by druids; and later still they were reputed to be places where fairies ("tylwyth teg" in Welsh) could be seen. Pentre Ifan was said to be a favourite place where fairies would gather to dance on moonlit nights. The strangest legend of all relates to Bedd yr Afanc, which is supposed to be the place where a fearsome water monster or "afanc" was buried after being caught and killed by local people under the bridge near Brynberian.

The Ancient Game of Cnapan

Another tradition is associated with the Ancient Game of Cnapan. George Owen of Henllys, Elizabethan squire and inveterate scribbler, described the game in detail in his famous *Description of Pembrokeshire* which was written around the year 1600. The game, a rough-and-tumble affair involving a hard wooden ball and up to 2,000 players, was widely played in various parts of Pembrokeshire, mainly in the Welsh-

speaking districts -- and Newport has a good claim to be Cnapan's natural home. Of the annual Cnapan occasions listed by George Owen the first, on Shrove Tuesday, was held on the sands of Traeth Mawr, Newport, between the parishioners of Newport and Nevern. Other games were played during the spring in other parts of north-east Pembrokeshire and the Teifi Valley.

Cnapan was a handling and passing game quite unlike the primitive football games played in many other parts of Britain. For a start, the gentry and yeoman farmers played the game on horseback, carrying and using cudgels, which must have added considerably to the hazards faced by those who were on foot. Among the latter were three categories of players: the "sturdy gamesmen" who were the equivalent of modern forwards, the "scouts" who were the equivalent of the three-quarters, and the "fore-runners" who seem to have had blocking duties rather like those of some players in American football games. After a stoppage the game was restarted by throwing the ball into the air as in the modern lineout, and there were prolonged episodes of mauling, rucking and primitive scrummaging. The skills of passing, tackling and evasive running with the ball were greatly admired, and it is clear that fresh players were brought into the fray at crucial times to replace those

who were tired. There seems to have been some awareness of defensive and offensive tactics, although with so many players involved the tactics could not have been very sophisticated!

It is not known when the game died out in Newport, but it is probable that no games were played at the venues described by George Owen between 1900 and 1985. However, the game of Cnapan was briefly revived in 1985-94, with an annual contest between players from the adjacent parishes of Newport and Nevern competing for a fine wooden trophy. There were various TV programmes featuring the game, and at the Gateshead Garden Festival in 1991 there was even a Cnapan international match which the Welsh players (all from Newport) won by a substantial margin since they were the only ones who knew the rules! In 1995 the game had to be abandoned, ironically, because of the increasing costs of personal accident and public liability insurance.

To this day a small group of Cnapan enthusiasts continues to argue that the game is the real forerunner of rugby football, and that the game which is now so famous worldwide started not at Rugby School in 1823 but at Newport in Pembrokeshire, some time in the fourteenth century ......

Waters Sacred and Profane

Like many old settlements associated with Norman barons and Celtic princes and saints, Newport has its fair share of wishing wells and sacred springs. Possibly the best known is the Wishing Well under a massive slab of rock on the downslope flank of Carn Cwn (Cairn of Dogs). It is not actually a well at all, but simply a seepage of groundwater which collects in a slight hollow in a horizontal joint in the bedrock. Traditionally the water is supposed to have had healing powers, particularly for warts and skin ailments. Also, there is a tradition that a brand-new pin, duly bent and placed with the right hand into the water and accompanied by a silent wish, will bring wish fulfilment.

The Treacle Well (Ffynnon Drieg) is alongside the lane which runs up towards Castle Hill. It is flanked by a brook with a beautiful name -- Nant y Blodau or Brook of Flowers -- which has its banks covered with violets, primroses, snowdrops and bluebells in springtime. Again this was supposed to be a healing well, associated in particular with eye ailments. The well was cleared out by the children of Newport School in 1970, but is now difficult to find.

Communal tap, College Square

Before the town was supplied with piped water in the 1930's, Newport people obtained their water from at least eight water-spouts, taps, pumps or springs. The word "pistyll" is normally used for a supply point of this type. Pistyll Dewi, Pistyll Samson and Ffynnon Gurig have saints' names, but normally the names simply describe the location or the adjacent property. There is an interesting cast-iron tap on College Square, and Y Pwmp (at the junction of Upper St Mary Street and East Street) supplied the residents who lived at the eastern end of the town. The most impressive water spout still in use is Pistyll y Cotham, at the bottom of Slade Lane, set in an arched recess and built originally for Cotham Lodge.

Further afield there are many other springs which are still used by local people for their drinking water in preference to the highly chlorinated liquid that comes out of their taps. There is one at Cilgwyn, close to the old corn mill and the candle-making workshop; because this spring is at the roadside, many people used to come in their cars to take its waters away in jerry cans, plastic bottles and assorted other containers. Sadly, the water is no longer safe to drink. There are at least another fourteen wells and springs in the parish of Nevern, including Ffynnon Penwaun in the village, Ffynnon Brynach near Carnedd Meibion Owen, and Ffynnon Bryncyn on the Nevern estuary. On the north slope of Mynydd Preseli. as indeed on the north slope of Carningli, certain springs have been incorporated into the present-day mains water supply.

Mills and Milling

Since it is not located in a deep valley, it might appear that Newport is not well suited to the use of water power. However, the old locals were nothing if not inventive, and the name "Afon Felin" (Mill Stream) gives us a clue that at least one small stream was harnessed and used for several centuries. The highest mill on Mill Lane was the Castle Mill (owned by the Lord Marcher) adjacent to Pont Henrietta Mair. It is now in a ruinous state, but in the Middle Ages it was used for grinding the corn of all the tenant farmers. Most of the water used to drive the overshot wheel came from the castle moat, which thus served as a millpond as well as having a defensive purpose. There was also a leat which carried water from the stream. The fields to the south of the castle have a herring-bone pattern of ditches, and it is now believed that these were used in an ingenious way to capture surface water and carry it to the castle moat, effectively draining the fields and keeping the millpond topped up at the same time. The mill was last used around 1932.

Other medieval mills included one that stood near Newport Bridge adjacent to St Curig's Chapel; one near the house at Rhigian and another nearby owned by one Thomas ab Owen; and Llwyngwair Mill which served the large Llwyngwair Estate. There were other corn mills also, for example at Cilgwyn, Yet-y-rhos, and in the Caman valley near Nevern Castle. There was a mill at Felin y Gigfran near Crosswell, and one on the Nevern River at Velindre Farchog ("Knight's Milton" or "Mill-town" in English).

At Pandy, not far from Llannerch in Cwm Gwaun, there are the ruins of the only known fulling mill in the area, where woollen cloth was beaten with drop-hammers to bind the fibres together in the production of flannel.

In the 1700's and 1800's Newport was an important centre for the Pembrokeshire woollen industry, and local woven cloth featured in the cargoes carried out to sea by the Parrog-based sailing ships. Some of the woven cloth came from a small factory near the bottom of Mill Lane, driven by a water wheel on the other side of the lane, with a shaft which passed over the road. The rest came from a larger mill at the bottom of the lane which produced flannel and other rough cloth until 1924.

The Court Leet, Court Baron and Mayor of Newport

There are some very old institutions in Newport, and among these the most important are the Court Leet and the Court Baron. Both have been involved in the administration of law and order in Newport and the Barony of Cemais for about 800 years. Broadly, the Court Leet was made up of local burgesses and freeholders who were originally responsible, through a "grand inquisition of jurors", for dealing with petty crime, collecting tolls and rents, looking after highways, and protecting the rights of rich and poor. The grand jury also submitted a list of three burgesses each year to the Lord of Cemais, so that he could choose one to be Mayor of the Town. The chosen Mayor was sworn in at the November Court, and thereafter through the year he would be responsible for the day-to-day administration of the town with the help of a bailiff and pound-keeper and four petty constables.

An old cartoon of Sir Marteine Lloyd, the Lord Marcher who died in 1933.

The Court Baron or Hundred Court dealt with matters relating to customs and tenancy agreements, trespass, slander, debts and land management matters in the Newport part of the Barony. It was held every other Monday, and down through the centuries it clearly had a lot of work to do! The old records show that many of the cases dealt with by the court involved disputes which would come under the Civil Law rather than the Criminal Law today; but through the centuries there have been many celebrated and exciting cases. No less important was the quiet work of the Court in determining grazing levels on the common lands of the parish, looking after rights of turbary (peat-cutting), piscary (fishing), the collection of firewood and building stone, and sorting out the ownership of stray animals including sheep, cattle, ponies and goats.

It is a testament to the determination of generations of Mayors, aldermen and burgesses in Newport that the ancient institutions mentioned above are still going strong. They have survived Nineteenth and Twentieth Century Acts of Parliament and other legislative measures designed to reform local government. Sometimes, Newport argued successfully for special exemptions, and sometimes (according to legend) Newport was simply forgotten about by the law-makers of Westminster! But somehow, by a combination of luck and good judgement, Newport is still designated an Ancient Borough. Its Mayor is still appointed by the Lady Marcher, who receives from the new incumbent a red rose as a sign of allegiance. The Court Leet and Court Baron still meet in May and September, and appoint new burgesses. And since 1964 a special annual court has been held towards the end of August to coincide with the Beating of the Bounds. This latter court is the only one which is open to the public.

Town Crier Rob Roughley

The Town Crier

There must have been a Town Crier in Newport since the Middle Ages, but records are sadly lacking. It is known that at least two of the town criers in recent decades were members of the Varney family. After a lapse of about 30 years a new Town Crier was appointed following a competition organized by the Chamber of Trade and the Court Leet in 1988. A special uniform in red, white and black (the colours of the Ancient Borough's coat of arms) was designed and made, and this is now worn by the incumbent on those occasions when official announcements are required in the town.

The Town Crier normally rings his bell and "cries" (reading from his special scroll) in the town centre, but in the past he has been called in to officiate at Cnapan games, carnivals and so forth at other local venues.

Ffair Gurig

Newport's traditional annual fair is dedicated to St Curig, an Irish saint who lived in the 8th-9th Centuries and who had some links with St Patrick. Nobody is quite sure what contact he may have had with Newport, but there was a Capel Curig near Newport Bridge, with a sacred well (Ffynnon Gurig) nearby. Possibly the parish church in the upper part of the town was also dedicated to St Curig before the Normans arrived.

The feast day of St Curig was originally 16 June, but when the Gregorian Calendar was adopted in 1752 the date was changed to 27 June. Ever since the Middle Ages the great fair was a holiday for local people, an occasion for merrymaking, buying and selling, and an occasion for the Mayor to raise revenue through the collection of tolls on livestock sales and from stallholders. There was much hiring of farm servants, settling of debts, and financial wheeling and dealing between farmers and merchants. The fair sometimes lasted for several days, and the Mayor required the attendance of all burgesses and the help of up to a dozen hired hands to control unruly animals and inebriated citizens.

Ffair Gurig, Market Street, c 1920

In the 1700's and 1800's the fair went through a number of phases of decline and resurgence, related partly to changes in the farming economy and partly to problems concerning the tolls levied by the Mayor on behalf of the Lord of the Barony. Neither the local burgesses nor the horse and cattle dealers who came to the town were happy about the tolls, and the old records are full of petitions and disputes concerning toll avoidance. In 1843 there was a move to start a rival toll-free fair in Maenclochog, and another in Eglwyswrw in 1851. There was even an illegal fair in Newport in 1862, and eventually the tolls were dropped.

As recently as 1935 the fair was a very large affair, with hundreds of horses, cattle and pigs lined up along West Street and preventing vehicular traffic from passing through the town. Market Street was lined with stalls selling fruit and vegetables, clothes and fabrics and a vast range of cheap-jack items for town-house and farm. There were games and amusements of all sorts. Sometimes the fair was so big that stalls extended down Long Street as well. There were even roundabouts and stalls in a travelling fun-fair in a field adjacent to Llysmeddyg.

Ffair Gurig faded away during the Second World War, but was revived in 1951 by Dillwyn Miles during his first term as Mayor. Nowadays it brings Ffair Gurig Week to a climax as a modest but jolly occasion on which local organizations and traders set up stalls on Long Street to raise funds for assorted good causes.

The Ancient Hamlet of Cilgwyn

Cilgwyn is a locality and a community rather than a clustered settlement. It is best described as a "scattered hamlet", with only one real cluster of houses around Cilgwyn Bridge and with maybe fifty or sixty dwelling-houses in the bad old days. The main physical feature is the valley of the Afon Clydach, which joins the Afon Nyfer close to Llwyngwair. There is abundant woodland along the river, but the most extensive woodlands are in the east, where Pentre Ifan and Tycanol Woods clothe the rocky slopes beyond the spur of Carnedd Meibion Owen. There are tors in the woods, but the most prominent ones are on the skyline above the top edge of the wood -- four splendid rocky prominences which are reputed to be the petrified remains of the last four giants to have inhabited these parts. To the west the cwm is protected by the mass of Carningli.

The dwellings were sprinkled more or less at random across the face of the land, some on sandy and gravelly hummocks and others on areas of thin acid soil. The majority housed labourers or peasants, some of whom had a garden or a small paddock to help them to eke out a living. Some larger houses were used by the tenant farmers and their families, and there were three or four more substantial buildings put up by those who owned land and who counted themselves as minor gentry. There was a church and a Baptist Chapel, and a number of skilled craftsmen including a blacksmith, a miller and a farrier. Although the community was tied quite closely to Newport it was not far from self-sufficiency, and many crafts including weaving, knitting, carpentry, candle-making, wood-turning, basketry and leatherworking were practised by people who could turn their hands to almost anything.

Echoes and Shadows

Money was in short supply, and bartering was commonplace. Cilgwyn split its loyalties between Newport on the coast, Pontfaen in the Gwaun Valley, and Brynberian to the south-east. The road from New England to Dolrannog and Penrhiw did not exist in 1814, and it was probably easier for the farming community on the southern slope of Carningli to get to Llannerch and Pontfaen than to travel to Newport.

After 1850, the rise of the merchant class brought newcomers into the cwm, and many of the old houses changed hands. With more cash in circulation and with improvements in the road network, Newport became more important as a shopping centre and the locals did less and less business with Pontfaen and Brynberian. Well within living memory there was a post office and two pubs in Cilgwyn, and the mill continued to operate until 1948. But there was not enough business for these little businesses to continue and thrive. Young people left the land, more and more families who spoke no Welsh began to purchase properties, and the Welshness of Cilgwyn was certainly diluted. In the 1970's and 1980's Cilgwyn became one of the great centres of the "self-sufficiency" movement, with key figures like John and Sally Seymour at Fachongle Isaf and Satish Kumar and June Mitchell at Pentre Ifan preaching the virtues of self-reliance to a worldwide audience. John Seymour was particularly influential, and his best-selling books attracted many others to the cwm. Even today Fachongle and Brithdir Mawr are famous for their residents who do things differently and who dare to challenge the planning rules...........

The view from Caersalem

Nevern and St Brynach

The little hamlet of Nevern, with its church, motte and bailey castle, riverside inn, ancient bridge and pretty cottages, becomes a "favourite place" of almost everybody who visits it. It is replete with old traditions, and St Brynach's Church probably has more folklore attached to it than any other church in Pembrokeshire.

It is said that the Irish saint Brynach was guided to this spot by God, following an unsuccessful attempt to set up a small monastic community in Cwm Gwaun. (He was driven out of the valley by devils, demons and unclean spirits.) There are several stories of the saint which relate to his time in Nevern, one of which is included in the second part of this book.

The Nevern Celtic Cross

One Nevern legend relates that the massive Celtic Cross which stands adjacent to the church belonged originally to St David, and that he was intent upon carrying it to Llanddewi Brefi in the Teifi Valley until St Brynach (a contemporary and friend of the patron saint) talked him into dropping it off at Nevern instead. Another popular legend concerning the cross relates that it is the landing-place for the first cuckoo of spring, which is supposed to arrive each year on St Brynach's Day, April 7th.

The cross is actually an eleventh-century memorial cross, dedicated to the memory of Meredudd ap Edwin, who died in 1035. It has extraordinary and intricate carvings, based on Celtic themes including plaits, twists and loops, all set in rectangular panels. It is made of local dolerite, but is in two parts, with the wheel cross fixed to the top of the pillar with a mortise and tenon joint. It was probably carved at the same time, and by the same craftsmen, as the Carew Celtic Cross which is at the roadside near Carew Castle. Some authorities think that the head placed on the Nevern Cross should have been placed on the Carew Cross, and vice versa!

The Bleeding Yews

Almost every visitor to Nevern knows the story of the Bleeding Yew Tree in the churchyard. Ancient yews line the path from the church gate to the church door, and several have exuded a dark red sap following tree surgery. According to one legend, the second tree on the right inside the church gate will "bleed" so long as there is sin in the world, as a reminder of the Lord's sacrifice on the cross at Calvary. According to another legend, an innocent man swore, during his last moments on the gallows in the village, that one yew tree in the churchyard would bleed as an eternal signal of the cruel injustice about to be done. He was executed, and the chosen tree has bled ever since.

The Beef and Barley Bequest

One of the strangest traditions of Nevern is connected with the Rodgers Bequest. William Rodgers was born in Nevern but made his way as a young man to London, where he became a wealthy merchant in Kensington. He purchased the Penrallt estate in the parish, and gave it to his mother and other relatives. When he died in 1806 he left a bequest of the interest and dividends on £800 invested, for the purchase of "good beef and good barley" to be distributed annually on St Thomas's Day (21st December) to the needy of the parish. In 1895 the proceeds were sufficient to purchase 505 lbs of beef and 50 bushels of barley, which was split by the Minister and Church Wardens between 124 recipients. After the Second World War there was enough money in the fund to buy one and a half beasts. In recent years the tradition has continued, with the meat supplied by the Davies family of butchers--Tommy, then Glyndwr and then Iwan. In 2002 only ten people came forward to request aid, so poverty in the parish is not what it was!

The Smelly End of Town

The least fragrant end of Newport has always been a small section of the estuary where Scholar's Brook bubbles out onto the mud flats. The town's first mortuary was built here, reputedly to contain the corpses of those who died in the Plague of the sixteenth century. The old building contained large slate slabs on which the deceased were laid out. Early in the twentieth century the building was brought back into use as a slaughterhouse by Mr ED Llewellyn, and later on the business was carried on by Tommy Davies and his son Glyndwr. The adjacent stream was useful for the discharge of blood, entrails and other body parts into the sea, which kept large flocks of herring gulls well fed. It was said locally that the rats around the slaughterhouse were bigger than cats, and that the eels in the estuary were as big as anacondas! Very close by was the town rubbish dump, which has recently been excavated by treasure hunters. One can only imagine what this district must have been like on a hot summer's day, at low tide...........

Nevern and the Ogam Code

Nevern Church played an important role in the deciphering of the Ogam alphabet, which was used for inscriptions on stones in Ireland and wales at the time of the Celtic saints. There are only about 60 memorial inscriptions in Wales, including those on the Vitalianus Stone and the Maglocunus Stone in Nevern. The former stands near the church porch, and the latter is now used as a window-sill inside the church. The alphabet was designed to be written along an edge of a stone using straight and diagonal strokes or cuts which cross the edge or lie on one side or the other. There were 20 letters, each consisting of between one and five parallel strokes. Confusingly, the letters could be written right to left, left to right, bottom to top, or top to bottom. Most Ogam stones have Latin inscriptions on them as well. It is reputed that the St Dogmael's Ogam stone was the one which first allowed the translation of Ogam into Latin in 1848, but the Nevern stones were also used in the attempts to "crack the code". The Ogam and Latin texts (normally personal names) are not always identical, and some authorities believe that Nevern's Vitalianus Stone contains "deliberate mistakes" and a secret code............

Matters Religious: Plygain and Pwnc

Two very old religious traditions have survived in Newport, one associated with the established church and the other with nonconformity.

The Christmas tradition of Plygain goes back hundreds of years. In the last century it was very common for people in the country districts to stay up all night on Christmas Eve in order to attend the Plygain service in the parish church at 3 am (or, more commonly, 6 am) before dawn on Christmas Morning. The service was in some places a prayer meeting, but more commonly it was a service devoted to the unaccompanied singing of special hymns written in the traditional Welsh metres and sung to old tunes. Another part of the tradition was the carrying of candles to symbolize the coming of the Light of the World; and this tradition may indeed be pre-Christian, with torches or candle-light used to signal the turning of the year and the return of longer days and shorter nights. Newport is one of the few places in Wales where the Plygain service still survives, attended by people of all denominations, and held in the Church Chapel at the top of St Mary Street. The ecumenical nature of the service is interesting, since the Church Chapel (which is now used for both religious and secular events) was used by the Methodists from 1799 until they seceded from the established church in 1811. The service is, as always, conducted entirely in Welsh. The tradition has been kept alive over the past 40 years by Mr Thomas Rowe Lewis and now by his daughter Mrs Aeres James.

The Pwnc festival is unique to this area, and has been associated with the local Baptist movement for over 150 years. It dates from the early days of nonconformity, when many members of the chapel congregations could not read or write, and so a method was devised by which they learnt parts of a particular chapter of the Bible by heart. Traditionally, the opening verses were learnt by the children of the Sunday School; the next verses by the young girls and then the boys; and the next by the young ladies and the young men; and then the middle aged men, the older ladies and finally the elderly gentlemen all in sequence.

At the Pwnc itself the verses are chanted in a manner which is quite unlike the melodious hymn singing normally associated with the nonconformist chapels. Some listeners have likened the sound to a sort of Gregorian chant, while others think it more reminiscent of a tribal war chant, rising wave upon wave to a strange, raw crescendo. After the climax there is sudden silence, followed by a series of questions from the "catechiser" to ensure that the congregation has genuinely understood the repeated words of the Bible.

The festival is normally held at Whitsun, and the four Baptist chapels that keep the tradition alive are Bethlehem (Newport), Caersalem (Cilgwyn), Jabez (Pontfaen) and Tabor (Dinas). The congregations join together each year for the Pwnc, and there is an element of competition between them in this strange and wonderful celebration of the Christian faith. Sadly, the Pwnc congregations are now much smaller than they were 50 years ago.

The Knowing Ones

The Newport-Nevern area had a great reputation in the past for its wise men, who served as seers or soothsayers, quack doctors, herbalists and even private investigators. They were also called conjurors, wizards or magicians, but they were definitely not in the business of performing party tricks! In Welsh, a magician would always be referred to as "dyn hysbys" or "knowing one" on the basis that he could foresee the future and look back into the past; and it was natural that ordinary people would believe him to be in touch with the spirit or supernatural world. Such men were always believed to have great leather-bound "magic books" full of charms, spells and incantations. Some were even believed to say "abracadabra" on appropriate occasions, and to be in possession of magic wands .

Magicians were held in great esteem as scientists and men of learning, and because they underwent long periods of training we can see them as the inheritors of the Welsh druidic tradition. They were not religious figures, and indeed they were themselves not opposed to churches or church-going. But in the days of the nonconformist revivals it was perhaps natural that churchmen should denounce them as being "in league with the devil" -- and as scientific knowledge increased it was inevitable that their influence gradually declined.

The most famous magician from the local area was Dr Joseph Harries of Werndew, Dinas, who is often confused with Dr John Harries, another famous magician from Cwrt-y-Cadno in Carmarthenshire. There are many stories in the literature about his prowess in removing curses, finding lost animals, solving mysteries, and healing sick people. I have turned Joseph Harries into one of the heroic figures of my *Angel Mountain Saga*, having given him the personality of a sort of proto-

Sherlock Holmes! In the late eighteenth century John Jenkin (Ioan Siencyn), the famous schoolmaster and poet of Nevern, was reputed to be a magician or conjuror, and there are a number of very strange tales about his prowess. Then there was Levi Salmon of Cilgwyn, known locally as "Dr Cwac", who lived at Plas y Ffynnon near Temple Bar and who was reputed to communicate with demons and to have special powers over animals. In more recent times there have been at least two other "knowing ones" in the Newport-Nevern area. One was an old man who claimed that he could talk to animals of all sorts and get them to do his bidding, and some of the locals were quite frightened in case he cast a spell over them. There is another whose family has always had a reputation for second sight, charms and spells. He seems a very amiable fellow, but it would not be a very good idea to upset him........

Parrog and the Sailing Ships

Parrog has been used as a port for well over a thousand years, and the people of the little community have always looked on themselves as somewhat "apart" from the people of Newport. Traditionally, this has been a place of sailors and sailing ships, and there is still a nautical feeling here, with salt in the air, people messing about in boats, and tall tales in the bar of the Boat Club.

Unloading a schooner, c 1920

Echoes and Shadows

The Parrog itself has been dramatically changed in appearance over the years. Originally "the port" probably consisted of nothing more than an open foreshore where small sailing ships were built and repaired, and where cargoes were loaded and unloaded. In Norman times the estuary was not so heavily silted, and access would have been easier at half-tide than it is today. As commercial activity and shipbuilding expanded in the Middle Ages, Parrog became one of the most important ports on Cardigan Bay, with exports of wool, rough woollen cloth, slates and salted herrings, and imports of coal, limestone, salt, wine, grain, tar, iron, soap, and a host of other necessities. The cottages on the sea front were built by fishermen, sailors and craftsmen involved in the local shipyards; and larger houses were built here and in the town by merchants and sea captains.

At last it became apparent that storehouses and proper quays were needed, but there were no major investments until the eighteenth century. Then four lime kilns were built on a spit of land projecting out from the shore, and between 1760 and the end of the century several storehouses and storage yards were built nearby. Part of the marsh was reclaimed. Work was started on quay walls and slipways, but the major work of defending the Parrog from the sea was not undertaken till 1816-25, when slates from the nearby sea quarries were brought in and used for the dry-stone walling which we can still see today. In its heyday the peninsular "port" at Parrog had two large storehouses and several smaller ones, a number of small cottages including one used by a lime-burner, and the lime kilns. One of the large storehouses was demolished in 1922 when the owner lost a wager, which resulted in it being dismantled so that the stone could be used in the building of the Memorial Hall! The other building was saved when it was bought by the Newport Boat Club, and subsequently converted and extended.

Ship-building was an important local activity, and there were two shipyards, one on the shore of the marsh on the eastern flank of the Parrog peninsula, and the other further up the estuary in the creek known as Bryncyn or Shiphill. Actually they were not proper shipyards at all, but simply level pieces of land just above high water mark from which launching could take place via a temporary slipway. Sometimes two or three vessels may have been under construction side by side on the shore, especially at the Parrog site. On average, a ship would take about six months to build. Only about a dozen ships were built at Newport in the eighteenth century, but after 1800 the rate of construction greatly increased, and well over 50 vessels were constructed over a period of 40 years. Mostly they were small sloops, brigs and schooners, generally less than 50 tons in weight and never more than 200 tons. The main shipbuilders were John Havard and his son Levi, but the shipbuilding work involved carpenters, sail-makers, blacksmiths, rope-makers and various other craftsmen, and the industry was of great importance to the local economy over a period of more than a century.

In the heyday of Newport sea-trading, around 1800-1850, over 100 sailing ships were based at the port, with many others calling regularly to pick up or deposit cargoes. Locally, the ownership of vessels was divided into 64 shares, and these shares were often owned by merchants, sea captains, and farmers. But the biggest shipowners of all were the members of the Davies family of Cardigan and Newport, who owned over 50 vessels as well as substantial property in Newport, Cardigan and St Dogmaels. Many male members of the family were mariners themselves, and several of them were lost at sea.

The coming of the railway to Pembrokeshire around 1850 signalled the end of the sailing ship era, but because Newport was remote from the expanding railway network the port at Parrog continued in use until after the First World War. As late as 1880 there were over a hundred shipments a year being handled, but after that there was a sharp decline, and after 1888 steamships began to replace the little smacks, schooners and ketches. By this time, silting in the estuary was a severe problem, and it was only on the highest of tides that vessels were able to reach the Parrog quays for loading and unloading. Normally, ships had to be grounded on the beach and serviced by a multitude of horses and carts during the hours of low tide. Among the last ships trading to Newport were the "Mary Jane Lewis" and the famous ketch "Garlandstone", and the last shipment was in 1934.

The Sea Quarries

One of the most interesting traditions in Newport is the use of the sea cliff faces between Parrog and Aberrhigian for the quarrying of shale and slate. These materials were used occasionally for roofing purposes, but because they were softer and more friable than the best Preseli Hills slates they were not very durable or waterproof; and so they were most commonly used as slabs for building purposes.

The sea quarries were operational over a period of at least 300 years, and in 1600 George Owen referred to the "black slate" as a major export item, sent by sailing ships to Haverfordwest, Tenby, Pembroke and ports in eastern Ireland. The main quarries were in Traeth Samuel, Chwarel Ffeiradon (Priest's Quarry), Aber Step and Traeth Brodan. They were owned by the Llwyngwair Estate, although not much is known about the leasing and working methods used in the quarries. The most intensive working was in the bays closest to Newport, where thousands of tonnes of material have been removed from the rock faces. Near Cat Rock a whole peninsula has been cut through from one side to the other, drastically altering the configuration of the coastline.

Walkers on the coast path can see many traces of the old quarrying activities, including small cuts and inclines high above the beaches (used for access, or to carry slate slabs up to the cliff tops), old working faces including occasional shelves and spoil heaps, and even small "docks" cut into the wave-cut platforms beneath the cliffs to facilitate access by barges and small sailing vessels. Most of the slate slabs were loaded directly into these vessels for transport either to Parrog or to Cwm-yr-Eglwys, where some cargoes would be trans-shipped into larger vessels for export.

There was very little mechanisation in the sea quarries, but black powder was probably used as an explosive to break up the rock face, and wooden gantries with block-and-tackle arrangements would have been used for shifting the largest slabs of slate. There were two great advantages that these sea quarries had over those located inland: the capacity of the sea to remove the slate waste from beneath the cliff faces, and the "soft option" available to the quarrymen of loading their shale and slate slabs directly onto barges or ships without any need for railway lines, tracks or wheeled vehicles.

Many of the slate slabs used for sills, lintels, doorsteps and scullery work surfaces in Newport and Parrog came from the sea quarries, as did many of the slabs used for building purposes. The sea walls, quays and slipways of the Parrog were built of slate and black shale from the quarries in the 1700's and especially during the major building works around 1820. The quarries were still working in the mid-1800's, but seem to have been abandoned well before 1900. Probably there were never more than 20 men working in the quarries at any one time.

Lime Kilns and Lime Burning

The tradition of burning lime in lime kilns goes back at least to Norman times, but the tradition of burning lime for the creation of an agricultural fertiliser in the Newport area probably began around 1500. George Owen, the eccentric local squire of Henllys, was a great advocate of lime burning, and he realized that lime could be used on the thin acid soils of the area to increase farm productivity.

Echoes and Shadows

As the Parrog developed as a port, small sailing ships called with greater and greater frequency, importing limestone fragments from the West Williamston quarries and culm from the collieries around Hook. These were the two essential ingredients for the lime burning operations, and rapidly became the most important of all the locally imported products. Before 1750 most of the lime kilns used in Pembrokeshire were crude temporary affairs, but with the mania for "agricultural reform" designs for solid permanent kilns were developed, and lime burning became an important local industry involving specialist lime burners and carters, and sailing ships devoted full-time to the limestone/culm trade.

Lime kilns were filled with alternate layers of limestone fragments and anthracite fragments from a loading platform which could be reached via a sloping ramp. Horses and carts were generally used for transport. The fire was lit from below and then maintained for weeks or months on end; the burnt lime was raked out through the kiln "eye", which also served to provide the draught needed for the combustion process. As the top surface in the kiln dropped it was replenished on a regular basis.

Shiphill Lime Kiln, not far from the bridge over the estuary

The lime was taken away in a cart and was then left in the open until rain caused a chemical reaction, turning dangerous quick lime into the much safer hydrated or slaked lime which could be spread onto the fields or used in the making of whitewash and lime mortar.

There were at least eight lime kilns in the Newport area, including four on the Parrog, one at Shiphill (Bryncyn), one at New Mill near Llwyngwair, and two on the shore of the estuary near The Marsh. There was another not far away at Aber Forest. Only three of the Newport kilns now remain, namely the impressive structure adjacent to the Pembrokeshire Coast Path at Bryncyn and the interesting "twin kilns" at the entrance to the Parrog car park. Next to these kilns is a little cottage which was built in 1788 (rather foolishly, on the downwind side) to house the lime-burner. It has recently been carefully renovated by the National Park Authority as part of the Parrog Enhancement Scheme.

The Herring Fishery

In Elizabethan times the herring fishery was of vital importance to the local economy, and vast shoals of herring moved around the Pembrokeshire coast on their annual migrations. Fishermen from Newport, Fishguard and St Dogmaels set out in pursuit of the herring shoals in the southern parts of Cardigan Bay during the autumn, using deep drift nets which hung vertically in the water with the aid of lead weights and cork floats. When the herrings were brought ashore they were measured by the "meise", comprising 620 herrings, and the sale income was split between the boat crew members with an extra share for the boat owner. The herrings were cleaned by the local women-folk and then salted down in barrels, often for export. Herrings from Newport and Fishguard went to feed the Elizabethan army and navy, and in the middle part of the eighteenth century there were substantial exports to Bristol and ports in Ireland and the Mediterranean. Later on, over-fishing, changes in sea currents, and changing tastes caused a decline in the industry, and it finally faded away before the First World War.

Seine Netting

There is a very ancient tradition of seine net fishing for salmon and sewin in the Nevern estuary. Probably the burgesses of Newport have been fishing with nets from the sandy beach of Traeth Mawr ever since the early Middle Ages, but as fish stocks have declined the number of

registered net fishermen has been reduced so that there is now only one license-holder. The seine net is up to 350 yards long and up to 12 feet deep, and the process of setting it and hauling it in involves a great deal of very hard work by a team of five men. During the 1930's there were two special black-tarred rowing boats based at the Cwm which were used for seine netting; they were both nineteen feet long, and were built in Aberystwyth. One was owned by Evan Davies and the other by John Selby. There were three main fishing stations, the best of which was "Y Llygad" near the river mouth, and the boats fished these stations in sequence, according to strict traditional rules. There were also other stations that could be fished on the flood tide. There was no fishing on Saturdays and Sundays.

Most of the seine net fishing was done on an ebbing tide. One man was put ashore on the beach, where he would secure one end of the net. The other men would then row the boat out around a half-circle, returning to the shore with the other end. The boat would then be beached, and the crew would haul in both ends of the net simultaneously, forcing the salmon and sewin into the central section. Finally this section was pulled onto the beach, with the lower part hauled in faster than the top in order to prevent the catch from escaping. Then the gleaming harvest was dispatched with the aid of a wooden truncheon called a "priest". Very often there would be no catch at all, but on other occasions 50 or more large salmon and sewin would be landed, ensuring a good pay-day for the boat owner and crew.

Madam Bevan's College

The Circulating Schools movement started by Griffith Jones in the 18th century made a great impact upon Newport and Nevern, but its travelling teachers were hindered by the lack of permanent premises. For example, on their visits to Cilgwyn and other farms and hamlets the travelling teachers (who taught both children and adults) had to use

John Morgan, teacher at Newport for 47 years

whatever premises they could find, ranging from church porches to barns. The move towards the use of permanent school buildings was held up while a bequest from Madam Bevan (the patron of the movement) was contested in the courts by various greedy family members. When her money was finally released in 1804 plans were immediately set in motion for a "Central School" to be established on College Square in Newport.

The school opened in 1809 on a site which is now commemorated by a slate plaque. The premises were spacious but spartan, with benches and desks but no blackboards, no maps, and no toilets on the premises. There were few books. There was room for up to 160 pupils, and the "college" was also used as a training centre for the teachers who would in the future spend their time "on the road" teaching for periods of three to six months at centres all over West Wales. Sometimes there were as many as thirty teachers in training, and Newport became a focal point of the whole Circulating Schools movement.

The scholars at Madam Bevan's School were taught spelling, reading and writing, with a strong emphasis on the scriptures. They were taught initially in Welsh, but if they made good progress they were also taught English and were given training in arithmetic. The Master of the school from the very beginning was John Morgan, who was given a cottage and garden on the other side of College Square. He received a modest salary and training in teaching methods, and he remained in the post for 47 years until his death in 1865. The school did not survive for long after that, for there was a move towards universal education; and following the formation of a local School Board a new and very grand school was built in Lower St Mary Street in 1874. This building is now used as the West Wales Eco Centre.

Over the Water

Over the centuries much effort has been devoted to local river crossings. In the early Middle Ages, when many pilgrims were following the "north coast route" to and from St David's, the stepping stones near Newport Bridge were in frequent use. Later on a wooden bridge was built, followed by a stone bridge with six arches, and this was still in existence around 1550. When the plague hit Newport about 50 years later, the locals became convinced that it was being carried into the town from the Nevern side of the estuary, and in a desperate and somewhat ill-considered action they demolished the bridge as a safety precaution. After that there was no bridge for over 250 years. Newport fell upon hard times, and there was no money available for rebuilding. Locals either had to wade across the river, or use the old stepping stones at low tide, or use the services of various ferry operators. Elizabeth Griffiths operated a rowing boat service on demand at Penybont, prior to the opening of a new bridge in 1892. Other ferry boat owners operated down on the Parrog, mostly rowing holidaymakers across to Traeth Mawr. They charged a half-penny at low water and a penny at high tide. As recently as 1920 there were five ferry boat owners still at work on the Parrog and another operating near Riverslea for the convenience of golfers.

In recent years the old iron bridge has been replaced by a new structure capable of taking heavy traffic. On the crossing itself it has just a single lane, and this prevents speeding traffic from disturbing (and running over) the bird-watchers who love to use the bridge as a vantage point for the observation of estuarine waders, ducks, swans and little egrets.

Henry Tudor at Cilgwyn

When Henry Tudor landed at Dale on 7th August 1485 with his motley army he was intent upon changing the course of British history; and he did just that when he defeated Richard III on Bosworth Field a fortnight later. It is not widely known that Henry and his army camped for the night of Monday 8th August at Fagwyr Lwyd, on the hillside above Cilgwyn Church. According to legend, he worshipped in the pilgrimage chapel before proceeding with his growing army towards Cardigan on the following day. Fagwyr Lwyd (which means "grey enclosure") is still marked on the map, as a small ruined cottage. It is close to a deep sunken trackway which was the medieval route leading to Newport.

Echoes and Shadows

The Lifeboat Station

Like any small town, Newport has its white elephants. The most prominent is the old lifeboat station at Cwm. It was built following a tragic shipwreck near Pen Catman in 1882. Two years later the new building was opened and a brand new lifeboat, named "Clevedon" at the request of its main benefactor, was launched. However, any visitor to the Cwm will appreciate that this site, at the mouth of the river, is not the best of places for launching a lifeboat, even at high tide. Because of this practical problem the "Clevedon" was called out only three times, during which it saved eleven lives. After 1889 it was not called out at all, and in 1895 the enterprise was abandoned and the lifeboat transferred to another station. The Cwm has been used for the town's inshore regatta for over a century, and is still popular as a little bathing beach.

The Highest Chapel on the Mountain

There were four chapels in Newport: The Methodist Church Chapel in the shadow of St Mary's Church, which reverted to the established church when the movement broke away in 1811; the Congregational chapel called Ebenezer, built in 1844 following a period during which it was linked to Brynberian Independent Chapel; the Baptist chapel called Bethlehem (1789, rebuilt 1817 and 1855); and the Presbyterian chapel called Tabernacle (built originally by the Methodists in 1815). As if that is not confusing enough, there were various other non-conformist congregations over the years, some of whom met in legal or illegal "meeting houses." One of the most charming buildings connected with nonconformity in the area is high on the mountainside on the road called "Mountain West" by some. It is known locally as Capel y Mynydd, and it was used for worship by a congregation connected to Ebenezer between 1875 and 1940. In recent years it has been converted into a holiday home.

Legends and Folk Tales

The Ghostly Parson at Berry Hill

David Griffiths started life as a tutor for the Bowen Family of Llwyngwair, and later took holy orders and was given the living at Nevern. He remained there as vicar until his death in 1834. He was a close friend of Richard Fenton of Glynymel, the great Pembrokeshire historian. He was a supporter of the Methodists, and was instrumental in the construction of the "church chapels" at both Nevern and Newport. He married into the Bowen family, and he and his wife Anne lived at Llwyngwair until 1810, when they moved out and took up residence at Berllan.

The couple had seven children, two of whom died in infancy. Their oldest son, George Griffiths, became a JP and Deputy Lord Lieutenant of Pembrokeshire, but he led a life of debauchery, and caused much sadness to his father David, who was a serious and god-fearing man. As to the character of the parson, we do not know a great deal -- but he had a reputation as a fiery preacher who stoked up revivalist instincts among the people of his parish and further afield. He was also somewhat severe and authoritarian, inspiring fear and respect in those who met him. He had always had a tendency to deep bouts of depression, and when his wife died in 1828 he was inconsolable. With his health failing, he moved from Berllan to Berry Hill, where his spinster sisters-in-law Elizabeth Alicia Bowen and Jane Bowen were then living.

His state of mind did not improve, and his desolation was increased by his inability, on the grounds of his physical ailments, to preach or to attend church. In 1834 he wrote that he felt "laid aside as worthless" and trusted that he would shortly be "released from this body of sin through the love of God." On a visit to his friend Richard Fenton he suddenly left the parlour, where Richard was seeking to comfort him in the midst of "a deep fit of melancholy and black despair", and was discovered, after a frantic search, hanging by the neck in the celler. He was cut down and revived, and when Richard remonstrated with him he replied that he was damned to perdition, and that "dark deeds require dark places for their execution."

He was determined to take his own life, and at last he succeeded, by hanging himself again at Berry Hill on 18 December 1834. He was buried in Nevern Churchyard, with more than 3,000 people in attendance.

For more than a hundred years after that, Berry Hill was haunted by the ghost of Parson Griffiths. When Air Commodore James Bowen returned to Pembrokeshire in 1950, after wartime service,, he moved into Berry Hill and was greatly troubled by the ghost. However, he obtained the services of a priest who had experience of exorcisms, and with the aid of bell, book and candle the restless shade of David Griffiths was finally laid to rest.

Pandemonium on the Parrog

This is the most delightful of all the folk tales of Newport. Old Daniel Thomas (who was called Daniel y Pant because he came originally from a farm called Pant) ran a little inn called the Parrog Arms, at Morawelon down on the Parrog in Newport. It was a miserable wet summer. The hay was mowed, and turned and turned, but it never dried and in the end it went rotten in the fields. Earlier on, Daniel had made several casks of beer in anticipation of the demand from thirsty harvesters, but since the harvest failed they never needed it. And to make matters worse, the beer started going sour in the casks, and Daniel could not even give it away to the thirsty neighbours.

That was the year when Daniel was trying to fatten up his sow called Susan. The weather must have affected her as well, because she lost her appetite, and whatever tasty morsels were placed in front of her, she just turned up her snout and walked away. Old Daniel became very worried, for she was as thin as a rake, with her ribs showing. But then one of Daniel's neighbours suggested that some of the stale ale mixed in her feed might whet her appetite. So Daniel agreed to try, although he was a bit sceptical about the idea. He mixed up a bucket of meal and stale ale, poured it into the pig trough and called Susan. She came over, without much spirit; but after a tentative lick or two at the magic mixture her ears pricked up, and in no time at all she had scoffed down the whole lot. So keen was she that she licked the trough clean, until it shone as brightly as the midsummer sun.

Well now. Daniel was delighted at this turn of events. He went back to the house, made another bucketful of the mixture, and filled the trough up again. And Susan finished it off for the second time. Daniel called his wife Mari, and together they watched her gobble down a third bucket of meal and stale ale. At last her stomach was so full that she could eat no more. Next morning Daniel gave her several more bucketfuls, and continued to feed her with the same mixture for several days. Towards the end of the week she was really beginning to look more like her old self, and Daniel thought that maybe they would have some decent Christmas bacon after all. He gradually cut down on the amount of meal in the mixture, until at last Susan was being fed on slops, skimmed milk and stale beer only. She became as plump as a mushroom, quiet and contented, and the neighbours were full of admiration. Indeed, Daniel thought it was a real pleasure to be in her company.

But one day things took a turn for the worse. Daniel was in the kitchen when his wife Mari came running in. "Daniel bach," she said. "Go down to the pigsty! I don't know what's come over old Susan. There's an awful riot over there!" So Daniel hurried down through the garden, and heard a strange squeal as he approached the pigsty. He peeped inside, and saw Susan rushing about in a frenzy. As soon as she saw Daniel she jumped straight over the wall and headed for him at a gallop. Poor Daniel fled back up the garden path, with Susan in hot pursuit. He just got to the kitchen in time, and slammed the door as Susan arrived. She attacked the door like an angry bull, with Mari peeping fearfully out of the small kitchen window. The old sow was just getting ready for a further charge at the door when she saw somebody coming along the quay wall. She became even more furious and charged straight at him. The poor fellow was so surprised that he did not get out of the way, and before he could do anything Susan went for his legs and threw him straight down into the field. He rolled over and over, yelling, and then got up and fled home along the Parrog. Then Susan saw somebody over on Traeth Mawr (Big Beach), and decided to go for him as well. She charged across the river and started trundling along the beach, but the man saw her coming and was able to take shelter among the bushes at the back of the sand dunes.

By now Susan was out of breath, and she ambled back across the river. The pandemonium had brought out all the neighbours; but as she approached they all fled inside and locked their doors. She prowled back and forth, searching for another victim. Daniel now decided that Susan had become a public danger, and he thought it best for all concerned if she could be shot, preferably from a safe distance. He didn't own a gun, but Ifan Dafis did, and he lived only a few doors away. So Daniel crept stealthily through the garden and along the hedge towards Ifan's cottage, hoping that Susan would not catch sight of him. Once there, the two men held a council of war. Daniel was all for shooting the sow, but Ifan said "I don't think she's gone mad. But I think she's got the deliriums on account of all that beer you've been giving her. I think that if we can tow her out into the bay, and keep her there for a bit in the cold water, she'll come over this spot of bother."

So a cunning plan was devised. By now the tide had come up, and the two men made a boat ready at the water's edge behind the old storehouse on Parrog. They also prepared a long rope with a loop on one end. Susan was prowling about over near Pen Catman, and when she came nearer, Daniel called "Biwcs, biwcs, biwcs". As soon as she heard him she came for him like a rocket, but at the last moment he jumped over the wall and slipped the noose over her head. She became even more furious, and went for Daniel and Ifan with her feet crunching on the gravel at the water's edge. But the two heroes leapt into the boat and pushed it off, rowing as fast as they could, out along the river channel and into the deep water of the bay, with Susan on the end of the rope, in hot pursuit.

Sad to say, it turned out that Susan could swim faster than they could row. She started swimming round and round the boat until it was spinning like a top. Daniel and Ifan were so giddy that they felt as if they were hanging upside down from the clouds. At last there was nothing for it but to let go the rope and escape back to the shore, leaving Susan swimming around out in the bay. When Daniel and Ifan returned to the Parrog there was a large crowd of onlookers, attracted by all the commotion. Daniel thought Susan was bound to drown, but she had a strange energy about her, and she swam back and forth between Pen Morfa and Pen Dinas over and over again, plunging and diving like a dolphin as she went. When it got dark she was still at it, and everybody went home. Daniel could not sleep, worrying as he was about his poor pig. So he got up at dawn and went down to the beach. There was no sign of Susan, and indeed she was never seen again. But the beach was covered in fish -- mackerel, herring, and pollack -- that had been frightened onto the beach by the porker diving and splashing in the bay.

Daniel and many other Parrog folk were at it for days, collecting up all the fish. Daniel had a cart and two horses delivering fish to Crymych, from where it was sent off to London by train. They do say that he made more money out of that one catch than out of forty years of farming at Pant.......

Phantom Funeral in Newport

William Havard owned a small shop in Newport and lived at a cottage called Penybanc. One night, having had various jobs to do after closing the shop, he was returning home very late. As he walked along East Street he was surprised to hear the sounds of wailing and weeping ahead of him. He stopped and listened, and suddenly he felt himself pushed backwards, as if by a large crowd of people, until he came to a wider part of the road. There the crush became less intense, and he was able to extricate himself from the "phantom crowd". He pressed himself against the hedge and became aware of a "toili" or phantom funeral procession going past him. He saw the coffin, recognized most of the mourners, and heard the women sobbing. What is more, he saw and recognized the local minister; and then he was even more surprised to see himself in the procession.

Much shaken by this experience, William hurried home and told his wife and two or three of his neighbours about it. Exactly a fortnight later, a man called Owen Griffith of Pencnwc died, and the funeral procession had a long walk into town. The mourners walked down Berry Hill, over the bridge at Pen-y-bont and into the town. As the procession passed along East Street it was identical in every respect to that observed a fortnight earlier by William Havard.

Ghostly Rebuke in Newport

Old Mrs Griffiths used to have a bakery and general store at Gwalia, in East Street, Newport. Sadly, her husband committed suicide, and she never got over the shock. She gave up the shop and moved to a house in Upper St Mary Street, and there she lived for many years until she died. She was a very severe and devout woman -- a pillar of the local chapel community, a stickler for convention, and a strict upholder of propriety. She would be seen every Sunday on her way to Chapel, dressed in black, with her bible under her arm.

When she died her house came into the ownership of a relative who decided to let it out to tenants. And so a young couple moved in. The man was from the locality, but the young lady was from Essex. They dressed rather strangely and had peculiar hair-styles, and in those far-off and unenlightened days they were referred to by the locals as "hippies." Gradually it emerged that they were not actually married, and that this was a situation that did not worry them in the slightest.

But one day the young lady came to see a well-known councillor who also ran a long-established ironmongery in the town. "We're very worried," she said. "We love the house, but we think it is haunted. Every now and then we see this old lady in the house. She stands on the landing outside our bedroom door. She is of medium height, has a rather severe expression on her face, and she is dressed all in black. She seems to be holding a book under her arm. Normally she just stands there for a bit and then she disappears. It's almost as if she's standing there giving us a ghostly rebuke."

The councillor felt the hairs stand up on the back of his neck, as he immediately recognized the description as that of the recently-deceased Mrs Griffiths. All he could assume was that the old lady, who was not a happy person at the best of times, was offended and angry in her spirit world at the sight of two happy young people living and loving together out of wedlock. The councillor agreed to help, and eventually the Rector of the parish came and conducted an exorcism which removed the ghostly old lady from the house. Now the house feels as friendly and warm as any other in Newport.

Scandal at Brynberian

Brynberian Chapel was one of the first nonconformist chapels to be founded in Wales, and the earliest congregation probably worshipped around 1690. It was then that the first building was put up. It was referred to either as an Independent or Presbyterian Chapel, with no links to the larger movements which later spread across Wales. In the 1700's there were great discussions on esoteric theological points, and on the means by which the congregation might be involved in decisions and by which a truly independent ministry might be provided for the faithful. In 1808 there was a rebuilding, and as the congregation rose towards 300 the chapel was demolished and replaced with a larger one (more or less as we see it today) in 1843.

In 1798 there was a great scandal at Brynberian when Stephen Lloyd, the minister since 1770, succumbed to the charms of "a lady of the neighbourhood." He had until that moment been a "wonderfully industrious" minister who had ministered to his flock in exemplary fashion and who had founded at least four other branches of the chapel in other parts of Pembrokeshire. But now, following his fall from grace, he was instantly dismissed, and although he subsequently displayed profound contrition and asked for compassion and restoration to holy communion, he had to face the judgment of the whole congregation. At the "big chapel meeting", when the time came for a motion of forgiveness and restoration of rights and privileges, twelve members stood in protest, so he was formally excommunicated. He died in 1801 without ever again receiving the holy sacrament.

This was the sad episode on which I based the climactic excommunication scene on pp 217-226 of the novel *Flying with Angels*.

The Lavender Lady of Newport Castle

Most castles have a reputation for hauntings, but Newport castle has a ghost who appears more benign than most. There are people in the town who claim to have seen "the white lady" on the lawns in front of the castle, but more frequently she is referred to locally as "the Lavender Lady". When Mr and Mrs Dean Shields were tenants of the castle, they would often smell lavender very strongly, even though there was no lavender in bloom and no lavender scent in the building. On one occasion Mr Robert Humfrey was sleeping in the castle, when he woke up to find an old lady standing at the foot of his bed. He was not at all frightened, and felt that she was actually a kind and gentle person.

A very old photo of Newport Castle in ruins, c 1850.

She may also appear in a very old cottage near the castle. Quite recently a young man named John, who shared this cottage with his girl-friend, was visited by his brother and his family. The visitors knocked on the door, and when it was opened by John the visitors saw three people and not two in the passageway. John turned and he also saw "an apparition" standing behind his girl-friend. The three people who saw it described it as "a misty or shady presence." John had previously assumed that there was some spiritual inhabitant of the cottage, since occasionally lights would be turned on and off in approved ghostly fashion.

Cecil Longshanks and the Toads

The farm of Trellyffaint, near Nevern, has been in existence for well over a thousand years. Once upon a time, a very long time ago, a young man called Cecil Longshanks lived there. He happened to fall ill, upon which he became persecuted by a plague of toads. At first he was simply irritated by them, but as the toads grew in number he became very angry. More and more toads appeared, and his anger turned to fear. Eventually he became quite terrified. His friends tried to help by killing as many of the creatures as they could, but the toads simply increased at a frightening rate. At last, exhausted by their efforts, Cecil's friends decided to haul him up in a large bag into a high tree which they reckoned would be out of reach of the toads. But poor Cecil could not escape from the pestilence; thousands and thousands of toads climbed up the tree, eating all the foliage and bark and eventually finding their way into the bag. Then they consumed Cecil as well, leaving nothing behind but a sackful of white bones which rattled as it moved in the warm summer breeze.

Family Trouble at Nevern Castle

The motte and bailey castle on the hill above Nevern Church was built by the Norman Robert Martin (Martin de Tours) in the early part of the Twelfth Century, probably as the original stronghold for the Barony of Cemais. Towards the end of the century the most powerful leader in Wales was Rhys ap Gruffydd, otherwise known as "The Lord Rhys". He was a clever politician as well as a great military leader, and he forged an alliance with King Henry which allowed relative peace in South Wales but which caused great resentment among his violent sons. In one of his astute moves he gave his daughter Angharad in marriage to William FitzMartin, who was then the Baron of Cemais. The couple lived contentedly enough at Nevern Castle, and Rhys vowed on all the sacred relics that he would leave them there in peace and quiet. However, the death of Henry in 1189 was followed by a period of political upheaval, during which Rhys revolted against the crown. Breaking all his oaths at the instigation of his "cunning and artful" son Gruffydd, he attacked his own son-in-law at Nevern in 1191, seized the Castle and evicted the young couple. Rhys then gave the Castle to Gruffydd, breaking another oath in the process.

Relations between Rhys and his sons were strained at the best of times, and three years later Rhys evicted Gruffydd and installed Maelgwyn instead. By now Rhys was finding it difficult to control his unruly brood and he planned to disinherit his own daughter, his grandsons and his two granddaughters. There followed a battle with his sons Maelgwyn and Hywel, during which Rhys was captured and imprisoned in Nevern Castle. It was probably at this time that the inner castle at Nevern was built, with a stone tower protected by a deep ditch cut into the bedrock. Rhys was locked up in the stone tower for the

A reconstruction of Nevern Castle, with acknowledgement to John Northall

greater part of a year. However, during yet another family feud, Hywel turned against his brother, burned the Castle and released his father. After this the attentions of The Lord Rhys and his feuding sons seem to have been diverted elsewhere; the damaged castle was abandoned by this unruly Welsh family, never to be re-occupied. As for William and Angharad, they built a new and more desirable castle at Newport and apparently lived there happily ever after.

Brynach and the Beloved Blodwen

It was a fine summer's morning in the llan or monastic community of St Brynach, at the place we now know as Nevern. The woodland birds were singing their hearts out, and after their morning devotions and a good breakfast, the brothers were going about their daily tasks as the morning mist rose from the grassy river banks. Now it happened that Abbot Brynach had a beloved cow whose name was Blodwen. She was larger, fatter, and more docile than the other cows, and was the best milker in the herd. Brynach had finished milking his cow, and his tame wolf was, as usual, taking her back to her meadow where she would spend the day amid the buttercups and sweet grasses and tasty herbs.

Suddenly the peace of the community was broken by a rough fellow who came running through the woods. He shouted that he wanted to speak to Brynach, and when the abbot appeared he said that he brought a message from his king, who had recently arrived in the area with his entourage. The king desired tribute from Brynach and his monks in the form of a good dinner and accommodation for the night. Brynach had heard of this king, who was nothing more than a marauding chieftain looking for trouble. Besides, the real king of the territory round about Nevern had already been converted to Christianity together with his sons, and he was the only one with any right to demand tribute from those who lived there.

So Brynach sent the messenger back to the king, saying that he would not take orders from a scoundrel, and would not feed or accommodate either him or his warriors. On receiving the message, the wicked king became furious, since he and his men had been travelling for many hours and were tired and hungry after looting and pillaging the countryside. He decided to teach Brynach a lesson, and sent scouts to discover whether they might be able to steal some livestock with which to fill their cooking pots.

The spies returned to report the presence of a magnificent cow, all by itself in the buttercup meadow; and in no time at all they had captured the docile Blodwen and led her through the woods to their camp. Then some of the men slaughtered her, skinned her and took out her entrails while others prepared a fire and filled the cooking pots with water. When all was ready the carcass was cut up into pieces, and the meat was put into the cooking pots over the fire. Then, amid noisy rejoicing, the men settled down happily to await their supper.

Meanwhile Brynach's tame wolf had gone as usual to fetch Blodwen for the evening milking. When it found no trace of the beloved cow, it ran back to its master's feet and lay there whining. Brynach knew at once that something was wrong, and followed the wolf back to the meadow. He and the other brothers searched everywhere, and eventually had to conclude that the animal had been stolen by the wicked king and his henchmen. Brynach was heartbroken, for he loved all animals and had a particularly soft spot for Blodwen. He did not know what to do, so he knelt in the buttercup meadow and prayed for divine intervention.

Brynach's prayers were answered in miraculous fashion. A few hundred yards away, at the king's encampment, the men were getting restless. No matter how they built up the fire and no matter where they placed the cooking pots, the water inside them (and the pieces of meat intended for their supper) remained ice cold. They fetched new water from the river and tried that, but the fresh water also refused to become even luke-warm. Then they decided to abandon the idea of boiling the meat, and determined to roast it instead, but still it would not heat up. At last, when it was pitch dark and when the king and his men were hungrier than they had ever been in their lives, they began to feel scared, for there was clearly some power at work that they did not understand. They made their way in a procession through the dark woods back to the meadow, where they found Brynach on his knees, still praying in the damp dewy grass.

So it was that the king and his bunch of ruffians pleaded for forgiveness and were converted by St Brynach. Having given themselves to God, they all made their way back to the monastery where they worshipped in the church. Then they were given a hearty vegetarian supper and were offered comfortable accommodation for the night. Next day the king and his band of good Christian men made their way peacefully back to their own country. On the way they passed the buttercup meadow; and there, peacefully grazing among the summer flowers and looking fatter than ever, they saw Blodwen the beloved cow, who had been miraculously put together again and restored to life.

The Voice from the Grave

John Jones (Ioan Tegid) was a poet and man of God, well known in Welsh druidic circles. He was vicar of Nevern between 1841 and 1852. He had a nice sense of humour, and he often used his uncanny skill as a ventriloquist to good effect. On one occasion Tegid was visiting a farmhouse in the parish when the conversation turned to the subject of the devil. He and the farmer and his family were sitting in the kitchen, not far from the great open fireplace or "simnai fawr". The conversation grew more and more heated, and the farmer shouted out that the devil could not possibly exist. At this, a strange sepulchral voice was heard coming down the chimney, saying "So I don't exist? Just you wait a second, and I'll show you whether I exist or not!" And just to complete the joke, Tegid shook with fright and fled from the house, quickly followed by the rest of the family.

On another occasion, the parish gravedigger was digging a fresh grave in Nevern Churchyard. Tegid had instructed the man where to dig the hole, but but for some reason he had gone to a different place with his shovel and was digging very close to another grave. Unknown to the gravedigger, Tegid came up from the vicarage and stood among the bleeding yew trees watching the excavations. Being a tactful man, he remained out of sight. But then the gravedigger was frightened out of his wits when a doleful voice came up out of the hole. "Oh, don't you come any closer," it said. "I don't want to be disturbed!" Tegid slipped away back to the vicarage. When he returned later in the day he found that the first hole had been filled in, and that the gravedigger had dug the grave in its appointed place.

Birdsong in Nevern Church

On the tomb of John Jones in Nevern churchyard the great man is simply referred to as "Priest, Bard, Scholar." At the foot of his tomb-stone there is a carved thrush. According to legend, Tegid died on a Sunday morning. As he lay on his death-bed, a colleague from an adjoining parish was taking his service for him in Nevern Church. Half-way through the bible reading his voice was suddenly drowned by the most beautiful song of a thrush. The whole church was filled with the sound, and the congregation listened spellbound to the soaring and joyful notes. The minister stopped his reading and listened too. There was no bird in the church, and yet the sound echoed everywhere, along the nave, to the roof timbers, and around the altar. At last the birdsong faded away, and the church service continued.

After the service was over, the congregation heard the news that Tegid had died in the vicarage on the other side of the stream, just a stone's throw from the church. It was discovered that the song of the thrush in the church had occurred at exactly the moment of his death. A few days later, at the vicar's funeral, a thrush was again heard singing sweetly at the moment of burial. And stranger still, when the monumental mason came about twenty years later to install a tombstone commissioned by Tegid's admirers, he found a dead thrush lying on top of the grave.

The Golden Idol of Trewern

Trewern is an ancient manor house not far from Nevern and about a mile from the cromlech of Pentre Ifan. It was owned by the wealthy Warren family. In the eighteenth century, and for as long as anybody could remember, the house had been haunted. Strange noises were often heard in the rooms, dishes would dance about in the kitchen of their own accord, and sometimes a lady dressed in a long silk dress would be seen. There appeared to be more than one ghost in the house, and although many attempts were made at exorcism the hauntings continued. The house was struck with misfortune, and in 1757 there was no male heir to the Trewern estate for the first time in 700 years. The last of the Warren family, old Edward Warren Jones, died a bachelor at Trewern in 1829, and the mansion fell into other hands. Finally, things became so bad that nobody wanted to live at Trewern, and it seemed that the house would be left to its fate and would fall into utter ruin.

But then, around the year 1840, the fortunes of the old house were transformed. The farm was let to one David George, a farmer and Baptist minister of Caersalem and Jabez. He had two old servants, surviving as best they could with few of the luxuries of life. But then Rev George suddenly acquired fine clothes and new furnishings. The old house was repaired and tidied up; new farm animals were purchased; and the servants were seen buying food, wine and other household items on a lavish scale. New farm buildings were built, and the land was improved through better husbandry. All of this needed money, but, try as they might, the neighbours could not discover where it was coming from. For several years Trewern continued to rise in the estimation of the neighbours, but still none of them could work out the reason for Rev George's new found wealth. The mystery deepened when it was noticed that he regularly left Trewern in his coach and stayed away for several weeks; and that whenever he returned there would be more lavish expenditure.

So the good times returned to Trewern. David George remained a tenant there and continued in the ministry. He became a substantial figure in local affairs, for example representing the Baptists on the Nevern School Board. Ready cash was clearly not a problem for him. He purchased Llystyn, Trenewydd, Brithdir Mawr and Ffynnonwen farms. With his new fortune he also built two other farms, at Trefoel and Dyffryn Benglog.

At last, in 1875, the farming minister died and the secret leaked out. It was revealed by an old servant that one of the resident ghosts of Trewern had told him of an "image of great value" sealed inside the wall of an upstairs room, immediately above the main entrance. A search had been made, and sure enough a large pagan idol, made of solid gold, had been found in a hidden recess. Rev George had then sworn his servants to secrecy, and had started to turn the image into money. Every now and then he would knock off a piece of it, melt it down in the Dolbont smithy, and set off with the gold nuggets to London, where he would sell them at the best possible price before returning with hard cash. In this way, over the years, he had sold the whole image, and nobody had been any the wiser. After the image had been found and disposed of, the ghosts of Trewern had disappeared, and there had been no more noises at night nor broken dishes.

There is still a belief in the district that the pagan image had been stolen hundreds of years earlier from an ancient Druid site among the oak groves of Pentre Ifan or Tycanol, which would account for the haunting of the old house. And there is still a conviction in the district that there are "Druid caves and groves" in the woodland..

Strange Bargain at Coed Cilrhydd

One fine June day around the year 1330, Cadwgan Ddu of Aberporth decided that he would travel to Newport to attend Ffair Gurig. His daughter Ellen begged to be allowed to go with him, and since she was a strong-willed girl she got her way. Father and daughter enjoyed themselves at the fair, but for Ellen enjoyment turned to rapture when she caught sight of a tall, dark young man in the crowd. He had a noble bearing, a scar on his face and the look of a man who had seen the world. Their eyes did not meet, but suddenly Ellen was head-over-heels in love. She made some enquiries about the good-looking stranger, and discovered that his name was Gwilym ap Owen ap Robert ap Eynon Fawr of Coed Cilrhydd , not far from Nevern. Not in the least put off by his long name (on the contrary, it signified good breeding), Ellen made further inquiries, and discovered that the object of her desire was the youngest son of a noble family of the area who had been educated at Oxford and at the English court. Further, it was rumoured that while in France with the King, he had defeated the French King's champion Sir Tristram in personal combat. On hearing this, Ellen's passions were of course further inflamed, and from that moment on she could not get Gwilym out of her mind.

Soon it was time to return to Aberporth, but on the journey home Ellen was strangely melancholic, and after that, for several days, she could not eat or sleep. Her parents were worried by her love-sickness;

but she would say nothing about the identity of her hero. At last she could stand it no longer, so she slipped away from her home and travelled back to Newport. Near Nevern she asked the way to Coed Cilrhydd, and found her way through Pentre Ifan woods to Gwilym's front door. She did not know what she was going to do next; probably she simply hoped for a sight of her beloved. She knocked, and was surprised when the door was opened by a woman. It transpired that the latter was Gwilym's wife, who welcomed Ellen and invited her in. "I have come to seek Gwilym," said Ellen. The wife said that he was away in the woods, hunting. Then, in a flash of inspiration, Ellen said "Madam, I have come to crave a favour." "Favours are not asked of me very often," replied Gwilym's wife. "But you seem to be a lady of good breeding, and yes, I will grant your request if it is in my power."

At this, Ellen explained that she had seen Gwilym at Ffair Gurig and had fallen madly in love with him. Then she said "My request is that I should be allowed to sleep with Gwilym tonight; after that, I give you my word that neither you nor he will ever see me again." The wife was flabbergasted, but she could not go back on her word, and she had to agree. Later on Gwilym returned after his day of hunting in the woods. He gave Ellen a warm greeting. Then his wife explained Ellen's mission, and said that she had agreed with the girl's request. Now Gwilym was flabbergasted too. As a man brought up in the courtly tradition he believed in fidelity within marriage; and at first he refused to have anything to do with Ellen. But at last, after pleading from both Ellen and his wife, he consented. So Ellen spent a blissful night in the arms of the heroic Gwilym, while his wife tried to sleep in another room. Then, next morning, Ellen went on her way, never to return. Nine months later she gave birth to a son, whom she christened Gwilym.......

John Jenkin and the Evil Spirits

John Jenkin (Ioan Siencyn) was initially a cobbler by profession but who then became schoolmaster in Nevern in the later part of the eighteenth century. He was a famous teacher and poet, but he was also reputed in the local community to be a conjuror or "Consuriwr" able to make contact with the Devil and his evil spirits. This is the best-known story about him.

One day one of Mr Jenkin's pupils asked him whether it would be possible to see the Devil. "You may see him", said the master, "if you have the courage for it. But I do not choose to call him until I have work for him to do." So the boy waited.

Not long afterwards, a man came to the teacher. He reported the theft of some money, and asked if he could help him to identify the culprit. Next day John Jenkin took the inquisitive pupil to one side. "Now," he said, "I have some work for the spirit world. Meet me at sunset if you will." So it was that he led the boy out into the wood and drew a circle on the ground, so that they both stood inside the circle. Then the master called an evil spirit by its name. A light appeared in the sky, and it shot like a bolt of lightning down to the circle. Then, as it moved around the outside of the circle, the conjuror asked it who had stolen the man's money. The evil spirit replied that it did not know, and disappeared. The schoolmaster then called another evil spirit by name; and presently they saw the resemblance of a bull flying through the air, as fierce and ferocious as could be imagined, and it too landed outside the circle. The mighty beast was asked who had stolen the money, but it did not know; and so it too disappeared.

By now the poor boy was almost fainting with fright, and the schoolmaster waited considerately for a while for him to recover his wits. Then he called for a third spirit. This time a spirit dressed in white came out of the shadows of the wood, and moved quietly around the circle. "Ah," said the conjuror, "this is better! Now we shall get to the bottom of this." And sure enough, the spirit spoke to the master in a language the boy did not understand. Then it disappeared in a ball of red fire.

After this, John Jenkin correctly told the man who had stolen his money, and it was recovered. But apparently the boy was so frightened by the encounter with the evil spirits that he was in poor health for many years afterwards.

Einon and his Fairy Bride

Einon was a shepherd lad who used to take his sheep across the great moor to graze on the northern flank of Mynydd Presely near Carnau Lladron. One day, in cloudy and misty weather, he got lost and wandered about for hours on the moor. At last he came to a hollow place surrounded by rushes, where he saw a number of fairy rings. He knew of the danger of these rings, for other shepherds had warned him about them; but try as he might, he could not walk away from then. Then a little old man appeared, and walked off into the mist. He was merry and blue-eyed, and looked harmless enough, so the boy followed, thinking that he might show him the path off the moor; and he was about to ask for help when the old man suddenly said "Sssh! Do not

speak a word till I tell you to!" So Einon kept quiet and followed.

In a little while they came to a tall standing stone. The old man tapped it three times, and then tilted it over. A narrow path with steps descending was revealed, and from it emerged a bluish-white light. "Follow me", said the little old man, "and no harm will come to you." So down they went, the old man in front and Einon behind. Soon the lad was amazed to see a fine wooded country with a beautiful palace, and rivers and mountains. Bird-song filled the air, and as they approached the palace enchanting music echoed between the marble pillars. They entered the palace and feasted on the most wonderful food -- but Einon saw no people, and the dishes appeared and later disappeared of their own accord. Now he could hear voices all around him. At last the old man said he could speak, but as he tried to do so he found that he could not move his tongue. This was very puzzling.

But Einon forgot about his minor problem when he saw a smiling old lady coming towards him with three beautiful girls. They were small in stature, but strong and graceful, with fair hair and blue eyes. He had never seen maidens more beautiful than these. The girls spoke to him, but still he could not reply. Then, much to his surprise, one of the girls bent down and kissed him; and all at once he began to converse in their own language fluently and wittily.

Einon stayed in this enchanted land for a year and a day, living with the three fair maidens in the palace and gradually falling in love with one of them whose name was Olwen (for it was she who had first kissed him). Einon thought that no more than a day had passed, for time had no meaning in the land of these beautiful and kind people.

But at last Einon felt a longing to see his family and acquaintances, and thanking the little old man for his kindness he asked if he could return home. The old King (for this is what he was) said "Wait a little while longer", so Einon did as he was told. But at last he determined to go. Olwen begged him not to leave, but when he had made a solemn vow to return on the first day of the new moon she let him go, loaded with treasures.

When Einon arrived home not one of his family or friends recognized him at first. Everybody believed that he had been murdered by another shepherd, who had become so afraid of the vengeance of the family that he had fled to America. Einon was saddened by this news, but he took care not to say where he had been. In any case there were great celebrations at his return home, and great was the amazement among the neighbours at his new-found wealth.

Then the time of the new moon arrived. Einon remembered his pledge and longed to see Olwen again, so he returned to the other country. There was great rejoicing in the beautiful palace, and before long Einon and Olwen decided that they wanted to marry. And so they became man and wife, but with no great ceremony, for the little people disliked celebration and noise. When the marriage was over, Einon wished to take his beautiful bride back with him to the upper world, and the old King and his people agreed to let them go. They were given two snow-white ponies, and off they went, taking with them as much gold and silver as they could carry.

They reached the upper world safely, and Einon no longer had to earn his meagre living as a shepherd boy. He was able to buy a large estate, and he and his wife lived there most handsomely. There seemed to be no limit to their wealth, or to their generosity with their neighbours, friends and relatives. At last a son was born to them, and he was named Taliesin. He was as fair and beautiful as his mother. People began to ask about Olwen's pedigree, for there was nobody as beautiful as she in the whole of Cemais. Einon never told anybody where Olwen had come from, but at last the whole district took it for granted that she was one of the fairy people.

Einon did not disagree with these rumours, and would say only that Olwen was indeed very fair, and that she had two sisters just as fair as she was. So it was that Einon, Olwen and Taliesin lived happily ever after, with the neighbours all quite convinced that Olwen had come from the land of the Fair Folk or Tylwyth Teg. And that is how the little people from the Otherworld first came to be called the Fair Folk.